CAPE EDITIONS 52

D1354098

Red Candle

Selected Poems by

Wen I-to

Translated from the Chinese by Tao Tao Sanders

JONATHAN CAPE
THIRTY BEDFORD SQUARE
LONDON

Available in the United States from Grossman Publishers, Inc.

This collection first published 1972
English translation and Introduction © 1972
by Tao Tao Sanders
Jonathan Cape Ltd, 30 Bedford Square, London wc1

CAPE Hardback edition ISBN 0 224 00701 7
Paperback edition ISBN 0 224 00702 5

GROSSMAN Hardback edition SBN 670-59106-8
Paperback edition SBN 670-59107-6

LCCC 72-81089

Printed and bound in Great Britain
by Richard Clay (The Chaucer Press), Ltd
Bungay, Suffolk

Contents

INTRODUCTION   7

I
from DEAD WATER (1928)
Confession   17
Withdrawal   18
'You swear by the sun'   19
What Dream?   20
The Ballad Singer   21
Dilemma   24
Don't blame me   25
Look   26
Perhaps   28
Forget Her   29
Tear Rain   31
The Last Day   33
Dead Water   34
Spring Light   35
Dusk   36
I wanted to come back   37
Night Song   38
Quiet Night   39
A Concept   41
A Discovery   42
A Phrase   43
The Deserted Village   44
Fault   47

T'ien-an-men 48
The Song of the Laundry 50
Mr Wen's Desk 52

II
from RED CANDLE (1923)
Red Candle 57
from The Death of Li Po 59
The Western Bank 60
Snow 64
Evening 65
A Poet 66
Looking Back 68
Defeat 69
Rhapsodical Thoughts 70
I am a young, strong exile 71
The Last Day of Autumn 73
Rotten Fruit 74
The Stream 75
Colours 76
from Scarlet Beads 77

III
UNCOLLECTED
Wonder (1931) 81

A NOTE ON THE AUTHOR 84

INTRODUCTION

Most people in the West know about the long clas-
sical Chinese tradition of poetry, but few are aware
of the twentieth-century Chinese poets who used
spoken Chinese, the vernacular, as their medium.
Amongst these writers, Wen I-to was one of the
most significant. His poems were produced in the
late 1920s, when he was a young man, and though
relatively few in number they had a considerable
impact on modern Chinese literature. Wen was born
in Hupei in central China in 1899. His birth coincided
with the disintegration of the old Chinese world
order. Much of the traditional classical learning was
rejected and the young looked towards the West for
guidance in all fields of knowledge, especially in
science, political theory and literature. Although as a
child Wen received a thorough schooling in the
traditional Chinese fashion involving considerable
memorizing of classical texts, he was subsequently
sent to a school in Peking, Tsinghua College, which
gave its pupils an education modelled on that given
in American schools and which also had a policy of
sending its graduates to American universities. Wen
later went to America for three years as part of this
scheme.

Having been taught, as part of his early education,
to write verse in the classical Chinese style, Wen
started to take an interest in poetry in the vernacular,
which was just beginning to appear, when he was

still at school. The movement for the use of the vernacular for written purposes was part of a much larger movement for national reform, the 'May the Fourth Movement', which started in 1919 and was named after the demonstration which took place in Peking in protest against the signing away of Chinese territory to Japan at the Treaty of Versailles. Although there was already a considerable body of vernacular literature in existence, it had never been taken seriously, and apart from collections of ancient folksongs there was very little poetry in the vernacular indeed. The classical language has a very different structure from the vernacular, and it was the language used right down to the twentieth century for all written purposes, as Latin had been in medieval Europe. The number of lines and of syllables in a line – and, in certain metres, even the tones of each syllable – were strictly regulated. The rhymes were made according to set rules of ancient usage and quite often had ceased to bear any relation to the way that words are pronounced in modern speech. Writing poetry was, therefore, an intellectual exercise which could be practised only by scholars, and so the new poets wanted to break away and create an idiom that rose above colloquialism without acquiring the overtones of classical formality. Many of the early efforts at this style of free verse read uneasily, and frequently they fell into exhortations and exclamations preceded and followed by 'oh' and 'ah'.

Wen's early poems, such as 'Red Candle', were not free from such faults, but later, after his stay in America, he began to evolve his own style. He came to believe that poetry should have a regular shape, and should adhere to the principle of uniform lines and rhymes which most of his contemporaries had abandoned. In place of the syllabic count, for which the structure of the classical language had been eminently suitable, he imported a system of metric feet, borrowed from English poetry. Chinese is usually accepted as a monosyllabic language, with one character as the basis for each word, but in modern Chinese this is only partly true, for most of the words are formed by joining two or more characters and in compound words some characters are stressed more in pronunciation than others. So in place of the long and short syllables in a metric foot, Wen worked on a system of stressed and unstressed syllables, which he organized into something akin to metric feet.

Wen advocated that poetry in vernacular Chinese should have as great a discipline as classical Chinese poetry had. This idea was one of the tenets of a literary society called the New Moon, which had its own journal and publishing imprint and with which Wen was associated. (Another prominent member of the society was the poet Hsü Chih-mo who had spent some years in England.) It was an era of literary societies in China which, with their journals, provided a platform for the young to propagate their ideas. Many of these societies were idealistic and reformist, and were as much concerned with politics as with philosophy and literature, but the New Moon writers were more specifically concerned with belles-lettres, earning for themselves the reputation of being elitist and dilettante. However, their concern for the shape and sound of the language, and their intent to forge a better instrument of expression out of the vernacular, made a contribution to the wider acceptance of the vernacular for all written purposes. Although Wen was strongly influenced by the West in his ideas about prosody, the content and the imagery of his poetry remained firmly in the Chinese tradition. References, overt or otherwise, are frequently made to earlier Chinese poets and poetry, and he was never alienated from traditional Chinese culture.

During Wen's youth, nationalism was a growing force in China, and his experiences in America also put him on the defensive about his country. Coming from a proud and well-educated middle-class background he was shocked and humiliated by the contempt of the Americans for the coloured races, and ashamed as well as defensive about the Chinese laundry-worker – the traditional image of the Chinese in America – for whom he wrote the 'Song of the Laundry'. A cultural nationalism was sparked off by this sense of humiliation, and although the bitterness passed, the defensiveness lasted the rest of his life.

Wen returned in 1925 to a China in turmoil. He had longed to return home and had inwardly built up a glorious picture of his homeland, but with his eyes sharpened by absence he saw all too clearly its general disintegration. The country was split up under the rule of local warlords who maintained themselves and their large armies at enormous cost; there was constant civil war and a widespread atmosphere of unrest. A dilemma rose in his mind : he was torn between a desire to help his country and a wish to lead a quiet life devoted to literature. The conflict produced poems of great intensity of feeling; poetically, the few years following his return were his most productive. His most expressive poem is 'Dead Water', a bitter symbol of China itself; in it he expressed his own repulsion and also his anger.

Though Wen was deeply concerned with the plight of the country and the suffering of the people, he cultivated at the same time the reputation of an eccentric aesthete; he appeared as a bohemian figure, with long unruly hair, who always wore an old-fashioned flowing Chinese gown, long abandoned by other men of his age and education. He professed a complete devotion to the arts, and his lectures to students proclaimed an engrossing passion for poetry. All this could have been partly a form of escape from a sense of impotence; poems like 'Quiet Night', 'The Deserted Village' and 'The Ballad Singer' show that he felt frustrated and unable to act. It was much later that he wrote to his friend and pupil, the poet Tsang K'o-chia :

> I only feel that I am an unerupted volcano, the fire burning me with pain, but I never had the means (that is, the skill) to erupt away the earth that holds me in and release the light and heat. Only a few friends who have known me a long time know that I have this fire, and even feel this fire of mine in 'Dead Water'.

The first few years after his return were not particularly happy ones; no suitable teaching post was available and he drifted from university to university in a series of unsatisfactory jobs, sometimes a target of student criticism. He had gone abroad to study art, but he had dropped this in favour of pursuing courses in literature. Now he began to turn his attention more and more to classical Chinese literature. *Dead Water*, published in 1928, was his last collection of poems and after this he virtually ceased to write poetry. His restless existence came to an end when he was invited to be a professor of Chinese literature at Tsinghua University – his old school, now raised to university status – and he remained on its staff until his death, working hard at his studies in Chinese culture on topics ranging from oracle bones to Tang dynasty poets; some of these studies have proved landmarks of scholarship. He became an immensely popular lecturer, as one of his students, the writer Feng Yi, recalled him, an emaciated figure with glasses in a long, old-fashioned Chinese gown, who would stroll into the overflowing lecture hall. He would go to the front and, smiling at the students, take out a packet of cigarettes. 'Would anybody care to smoke?' he would say. The audience would laugh but no one ever had the courage to accept. Then he would pick one out himself and, having lit it, would start on his lecture by declaiming a quotation from his text. He then held the audience entranced until he stopped, usually long after the scheduled time, so that when the students streamed away 'the moon was bright'. This enthusiasm for classical Chinese literature might appear to be against the trend of the time, but though Wen continued to believe in reform, he was not prepared to reject the Chinese tradition altogether. He said, in later life, that he had taken up the study of the Chinese classics in order to be able to refute them, but this was perhaps a subsequent rationalization.

If life in China had continued uneventfully, Wen might have remained merely a distinguished literary figure, but the Sino-Japanese war precipitated his development into something more. The Japanese occupied north China in 1937, and he was evacuated to the interior with the University. On his journey there, he passed through some of the most under-developed parts of China, whose abysmal poverty shocked him deeply. During the war, he suffered all the privations of wartime life, which impressed on him the need for China's complete reformation. This time he committed himself by taking an active part in politics. He joined the People's Democratic League, a minority third party consisting mainly of liberals and intellectuals who took up a position between the communists on the one hand and the nationalists on the other. He made speeches and wrote articles for the party journal, and his already well-established reputation amongst students made him highly effective. The war came to an end, the evacuated gradually returned to their homes, but Wen continued his association with the People's Democratic League campaign for liberal reforms. Wen the political activist had taken over entirely from Wen the literary man. He never ceased to teach, but his lectures became increasingly slanted towards revolutionary ideals. The poets he admired most were politically committed revolutionaries, in particular his contemporary, Tien Chien, whose verse in short staccato lines, as Wen said, reflected the 'drum beat' of a new life. The League became increasingly unpopular with the government, and prominent members were assassinated. On July 15th, 1946, at a public meeting preceding the funeral of one of the dead leaders, Wen made an impassioned speech denouncing the government. That same evening as he was leaving the office of the League in the company of his son, he was shot at by gunmen and killed.

T.T.S.

I

from DEAD WATER (1928)

Confession

I am not fooling you, I am not a poet,
Although what I love is the purity of white stones,
Blue pines and the great sea, the sun setting on the
    backs of ravens,
The dusk cross-woven with the wings of bats.
You know that I love heroes, and love high mountains,
And I love our country's flag beckoning in the wind,
And chrysanthemums in a spectrum from yellow to
    dark brown.
Remember that my sustenance is but a pot of bitter
    tea!

But there is another I – Are you afraid? –
Thoughts like flies, crawling in the rubbish bins.

Withdrawal

That day if Fate can only release us,
Don't be afraid; although we must walk through a
 dark cave,
Go bravely, let me take your hand,
There is no need to ask from where blows that gust of
 dank wind.

Only remember what I have said today, keep in your
 heart
The handful of tenderness, the petals of kisses, keep
 those flames of laughter in your heart,
Pick them all up, without losing one – remember my
 words,
Pick them up, and the string of coral-coloured heart-
 beat.

I am sorry you have been grieved today – thirsty
 heart longing for heart –
That time I should have let you pick them up, pick
 them to your heart's content.
Pick up the precious time that we have lost today.
Those few mottled fading petals that were our love,
Pick them up, and put them on.
                    You have put on the halo of love,
Let us go on again, whether it is Hell or Heaven.

'You swear by the sun'

You swear by the sun, and call on the horizon's cold
    swans,
And talk about your constancy. Very well, I believe
    you completely,
And even those tears blossoming from your hot pas-
    sion don't surprise me,
But if you were to talk of the constancy of seas and
    mountains ...
Then I should die with laughter. Isn't this instant
Enough to make me drunk with happiness? Why talk
    of 'forever'?
Love? You know that I have no more than a puff of
    breath of desire.
Hurry and grip my heart! Hurry! But you are going,
    you're going ...

I've long anticipated that trick – it isn't any change-
    fulness –
'Forever' was long ago given to someone else, only the
    chaff is my share.
Your youth is what the others have received – your
    imperishable spring.
You don't believe me? If one day Death were to show
    you his warrant,
Would you go? Go, go to his embrace,
And talk to him about your constancy like the sea
    and the mountain.

What Dream?

A row of wild geese, harassed, crossed the Milky Way,
The birds' wail pierced through her heart,
'My man, my man,' she sighed,
'Where are you? From where are you calling me?'

Dusk ushered in fear, pressed hard straight upon her,
A ball of pain sank down heavily on her heart,
'Heaven, oh heaven,' she cried,
'What really is it? What really is the meaning of
    this?'

The road was so long, and the journey at night,
She stood hesitating at the threshold of life and
    death,
'Despondency, weary despondency,' she thought,
'I shall for ever, for ever put an end to you.'

Decision was written on her face – a decisive ease.
Suddenly there came a howl from the cradle, like an
    alarm bell
'My child, my child,' she wept,
'What kind of, what kind of a dream have I dreamt?'

The Ballad Singer*

I slung a drum of leopard-skin at my side,
　　Beating it I travelled throughout the world.
I have sung songs of every shape and kind,
　　And satiated myself on the endless applause.

A corner of the slanting sun hung upside down on the
　　　　eaves,
　　I tip-toed in my straw sandals and strode into my
　　　　village.
'Where is that song of our own?'
　　She hurried forward with a wave of happiness.

I can sing of heroes, I can sing of warriors,
　　That song of girl and lover I can also sing,
If you were to ask about our very own song,
　　Heaven knows, I am at my wits' end to say.

But I swallowed my grief and called to her,
　　'Quickly bring me my three-stringed fiddle, be
　　　　quick,
I'm tired of the noise of this old drum, I want
　　The strings to play my song.'

I first played a flock of white doves in a frosty wood,
　　Their coral claws treading on a heap of yellow
　　　　leaves,

* *Ta-ku-shih*: an itinerant singer and story-teller. Such
people provided a form of entertainment popular in north
China.

Then you can hear a cricket crying in the crack in
   the stone
   Suddenly turn into a sound of cold rain lashing the
   wooden gate,

Rain that will never stop falling, tears that will never
   stop flooding ...
   I cried out, 'Lady,' and threw away my fiddle,
'What shall we take to sing about today?
   My songs have long since turned to tears which
   flowed away.

'What? Can you not lift your head either?
   What shall we do about it? What shall we do?
Come, come here, you must let me kiss dry
   The grief that I shook out.

'Only let me stare at you like this, lady,
   Like the cold palm looking at the moon,
Let me praise you in silence,
   But I shall never think of any song to sing.

'Although it was an axe which carved out the love
   branch,
   Look, its shape hasn't been distorted at all,
My lovable one, don't be resentful of me.
   I do not blame the hand that waved the axe.

'Don't be suspicious, and ask no questions,
   When the mountain spring has arrived at the
   bottom of the well, where else can it flow?
I know that you will never raise a ripple
   I want you always to moisten my throat for song.

'Supposing the last hope was denied the lonely boat,
  Supposing you refused me my harbour,
I shall fight with the wind and waves and return in
    the evening,
  Who is my home, who is my refuge?

'But, lady, before you,
  Let me dispense with drum and fiddle,
We really have no songs suitable for singing,
  Since we are neither lovers nor heroes.'

Dilemma

Supposing the slanting sunlight on flowing water
Slowly comes and slowly goes;
Supposing at that time it is not that I don't keep you
But that my heart will not be obedient to me.

Supposing it is the grey-coloured dusk again,
Full of the hidden wings of bats;
Supposing at that time it is not that I do not long for
   you
But that then the heart will not be able to think of
   anything at all.

Supposing when falling leaves scatter like fleeing sol-
   diers
And dark shadows peer before my window;
Supposing this heart is no longer mine,
Woman, how can it think of you?

Supposing the autumn night is so lonely too ...
Eh? Who is this whispering in my ear,
This clearly is not your voice, woman;
Supposing that she insists on my surrendering to her.

Don't blame me

Don't blame me.
It wasn't much to begin with;
Life is the meeting of floating duckweeds,
Like duckweeds let them pass each other by.
Don't blame me.

Don't question me.
Tears are waiting at the corner of my eyes,
It only needs you to speak one word,
One word will make them fall.
Don't question me.

Don't rouse me.
Don't think to light a fire on ashes,
My heart has long since fallen from tiredness,
It's best to let it sleep,
Don't rouse me.

Don't touch me.
What are you thinking of? What?
We're only floating duckweeds meeting,
We should lightly pass each other by,
Don't touch me.

Pay no more attention to me.
From now on fix another lock to the door.
Don't ever knock on the wrong one again.
This time let it be my fault.
Pay no more attention to me.

Look

Look, the sun like a spring silkworm roused from
    sleep
Spits endless rays like yellow silk all day.
Look how the sunbathing redbreast perches on the
    telegraph pole,
Sweetly sleeping brocaded ducks are moored beside
    the willow root.

Before your eyes are laid the treasures of spring again,
Friends, enjoy what is in front of your eyes;
You have eyes, look again at the folds of the blue
    hills,
But don't pine for your home beyond the mountains.

Listen to the mottled sparrow hymning spring on the
    tip of that branch,
You must dry your tears and sing a song with him.
Friend, homesickness is the most pitiless demon,
He can make the spring light before your eyes change
    into a desert.

Look how the spring breeze has freed the ice-locked
    cold stream,
White teeth midway in the stream are lightly rinsed
    by ripples,
Fine grass has again knitted a luxuriant green,
The white birch branches are waving tiny silver flags.

Friend, by the time you see the spring of your home-
    land,
I fear that spring will have been wasted and so will
    you.
Do not pine for your home, friend,
For home is a thief; he can steal your heart away.

Perhaps

Perhaps you are really worn out with crying;
Perhaps, perhaps you want to sleep a bit.
Then let the night hawks not cough,
The frogs not croak, the bats not fly,

I won't let the sunlight stir the curtain of your eyes,
I won't let the breeze brush your eyebrows,
Nobody at all will be able to wake you.
I shall stretch an umbrella of pine trees to guard
    your sleep,

Perhaps you are listening to the earthworms turning
    the clay,
And hear the roots of young grasses suck water,
Perhaps this kind of music you hear
Is more beautiful than the cursing voices of men;

Then, first shut your eyelids tightly;
I'll let you sleep, I'll let you sleep.
I'll gently cover you with brown earth.
I'll let the ashes of paper money float softly around.*

* Paper money is burnt for the dead.

Forget Her

Forget her like a forgotten flower,
      The morning clouds on the petal,
      The scent from the heart of the flower –
Forget her like a forgotten flower!

Forget her like a forgotten flower!
      Like a dream scene in the spring breeze,
      Like the striking of a clock in a dream,
Forget her like a forgotten flower!

Forget her like a forgotten flower!
      Listen how well the crickets sing,
      Look how tall the grass grows on the grave;
Forget her like a forgotten flower!

Forget her like a forgotten flower!
      She has already forgotten you,
      She cannot remember anything at all,
Forget her like a forgotten flower!

Forget her like a forgotten flower!
      Youth is a really good friend,
      He'll make you old by tomorrow,
Forget her like a forgotten flower!

Forget her like a forgotten flower!
      If anyone were to ask,

Then say there was no such person;
Forget her like a forgotten flower!

Forget her like a forgotten flower!
        Like a dream scene in the spring breeze,
        Like the striking of a clock in a dream,
Forget her like a forgotten flower!

Tear Rain

In the time of the spring of his life
He sheds tears that cry his hunger and cold;
That is the spring shower, ice-thawing and life-
reviving,
Which also presages the grief of life.

The tears of his youth are continuous gloomy rain,
That secretly ripen the bitter-sour yellow plum;
Now the black clouds gather, thunder and lightning
join,
His tears are like the downpour of summer rain.

In the bewilderment of the middle road, the stumbling
of the aged,
He knows that the bitter tears of middle age are
heavier,
The tears of middle age are like lingering autumn
rain,
The night-long dirge knocking on the wu-t'ung tree.*

Who says that the end of the winter of life has no
tears?
The tears of old age are the fusion of sadness;

* This echoes a line from the poem 'Song of Everlasting
Regret' by Po Chu-i (772–846), which describes the aged
Emperor Hsüan-tsung, moved by the sound of rain in autumn
playing on the wu-t'ung trees, recalling his happier days with
his consort Yang Kuei-fei. It is also the title of a Yüan drama
of the same story.

He still has a handful of crystallized tears of old age,
Which will blossom into a skyful of flowers that make
    men sad.

The Last Day

The water from the dew gurgles in the pipe,
The green tongue of banana leaves licks the window-
    pane,
The whitewashed walls on all four sides are retreat-
    ing,
Alone I cannot fill such a large room.

In my heart burns a bowl of fire,
Quietly I wait for the arrival of a far-away guest,
I feed the fire with cobwebs and mice-droppings,
And use the armour of mottled snakes for firewood.

The cockcrow is pressing, in the bowl is a heap of
    cinders,
A gust of dank wind steals to touch my mouth,
So the guest is standing before my eyes.
I clear my throat and follow the guest.

Dead Water

Here is a ditch of hopeless dead water,
The fresh breeze would not even raise half a ripple.
One might as well throw in a few more tins and scraps
     of metal
And why not pour in your left-over food and gravy.

Perhaps the green of the copper will turn into emerald,
Rust on the tin cans emerge as petals of peach blos-
     som;
Then let grease weave a layer of patterned muslin,
And bacteria brew vapours of coloured clouds.

Let the dead water ferment into a gully of green wine,
Floating pearl-like crowds of white foam;
The laughter of small pearls will change them to large
     pearls
Broken by mosquitoes to steal the alcohol.

Even a ditch of hopeless dead water
Can boast of some ornaments.
If the green frogs can't bear the silence,
Then we can say that the dead water can sing.

Here is a ditch of hopeless dead water,
This cannot be a place where beauty lives,
Better let ugliness cultivate it,
And see what kind of world comes of it.

Spring Light

As quiet as in a meditation were the hawthorn,
The coral berries that its thick leaves could not cover,
And the oleander; in the morning light sat a yogi
  sparrow.
Spring light climbed over the green leaves one by one.
A shaft of sunlight striking the ground flashed before
  my eyes,
As if a thousand golden arrows flew out of my eyes,
The rustling of wings penetrated my ears,
As though a flock of angels were patrolling the air ...

Suddenly from the deep lane came the sound of a clear
  flute:
'Have pity, have pity on a blind man, ladies and
  gentlemen!'

Dusk

Dusk is a slow clumsy black ox
Step by step walking down the western hill;
You mustn't lock up the city gate too early
Always wait for the black ox to come into the city
    pen.

Dusk is a mysterious black ox,
I don't know of which world he is the god –
Every day the moon sees him into the city
In the morning the sun leads him up the western
    hill again.

I wanted to come back

I wanted to come back,
Whilst your clenched hand was like an iris in bud,
Whilst your soft hair was just like soft silk,
Whilst heavenly light burned in your eyes,
I wanted to come back.

I didn't come back,
Whilst your footsteps were like moving oars in the wind,
Whilst your heart beat on the windowpane like a senseless fly,
Whilst your laughter held silver bells.
I didn't come back.

I should have come back,
When the coma descended on your eyes,
When the dark wind blew out the lamp,
When the cold hand plucked you away,
I should have come back.

I have come back,
When the glowworm holds its lantern to shine on you,
When the cricket chirps beside your ears,
When you are sleeping with earth in your mouth.
I have come back.

Night Song

The scabby toad gave a shiver,
Out of the mound of yellow earth crawled a woman,
No dark shadow could be seen beside the woman,
Although the moonlight was very bright.

Out of the mound of yellow earth crawled a woman,
But there was no trace of a crack on the mound of
 yellow earth;
She didn't even disturb an earthworm,
Or break a thread of spider's web.

In the moonlight sat the woman;
The woman seemed as though she was young,
Her scarlet dress fearful like blood,
Long hair loosely scattered over her back.

The woman was shrieking, beating her breast,
The scabby toad just gave a shiver,
The lone cock in the far village gave a crow,
There was no woman to be seen on the mound of
 yellow earth.

Quiet Night

originally called A Leaping Heart

The lamp, the four walls bleached by its light,
The good table and chairs as close as friends,
Whiffs of sweet smell from an old book,
Pure teacups white like a virgin,
The sucking baby in his mother's arms,
The snores of my elder boy assuring me that he is
    well ...
The mysterious quiet night, this good-natured peace.
In my throat I sing a thanksgiving.
But the song turns to curses,
Quiet night, I cannot, I cannot accept your bribery.
Who prizes the peace within your square foot of
    walls!
My universe has still wider frontiers.
These four walls cannot cut off the clamour of wars,
How can you stop my heart from leaping?
You must stuff my mouth with sand and mud,
If it can only sing about an individual's welfare!
You must let this head be hollowed by field-mice,
And let this mass of flesh and blood feed worms,
If it is only for a cup of wine and a book of verse,
The leisure brought by the ticking clock,
That I don't hear the groans of your neighbours,
That I don't see the trembling shadows of the widows
    and orphans,

The spasms in the trench, the lunatic gnawing his bed,
And all sorts of pain between the millstones of life.
Luck, I cannot accept your bribery,
My universe is not this square foot within these walls,
Listen, another volley of cannons, the roar of the god
of death.
Quiet night, how can you stop my heart from leap-
ing?

A Concept

You perpetual mystery, you beautiful lie,
You obstinate questioning, you ray of golden light,
A touch of intimacy, a flame of fire,
A floating cry, what are you?
I am not in doubt; this is my true karma,
I know that the ocean does not lie to its waves.
If the music is in harmony, I shouldn't complain
   about the words of the song.
Ah, power of tyranny, you have overcome me,
You have overcome me, you many-coloured rain-
   bow –
The memory of five thousand years, do not move,
Now I only ask how I might hold you tightly ...
You are so savage, so beautiful.

A Discovery

I came, I screamed, scattering blood and tears,
'This is not my China, no, no!'
I came because I heard you call me;
Whipping up on the whirlwind of time, holding a
    torch high,
I came not knowing that I should be robbed of my
    happiness.
What I saw was a nightmare, how can it be you?
It is terror, it is a nightmare hanging on the cliffs,
It is not you, it is not my love!
I demand of the sky, threaten the winds,
I ask (fists beating the earth's bare bosom),
I never find out, I weep and shriek for you,
I spit out a heart – in my heart.

A Phrase

There is a phrase that spoken will bring disasters,
There is a phrase that can ignite fires.
No matter that it hasn't been uttered in five thousand
    years,
Can you fathom the quiescence of a volcano?
Perhaps it has been suddenly possessed by a demon,
Suddenly a thunderbolt came out of the blue sky,
              With an explosion :
        'Our China !'

How can I voice this phrase today ?
Don't you believe that iron trees will bear blossoms ?
Then you must listen to these words :
Wait till the volcano can no longer endure the
    quiescence.
Then don't tremble, be at a loss, or stamp your foot,
Wait till there is a thunderbolt from the blue sky,
              With an explosion :
        'Our China.'

The Deserted Village

For seventy miles between the towns of Lin-huai-kuan and Liang-yüan-chen it is completely deserted. The villages on either side of the road where people lived are quite empty. The tools and furniture of the farmers are tied together with ropes and dumped into nearby water-filled paddy fields, to prevent them from being burnt. The doors and windows are all gone; some of the gaps are stopped up with coffins or stones. When night falls, there is not a single light to be seen. Chickens, dogs, pigs, etc., feed in the wild, with no one to look after them. Here and there roses and peonies bloom in corners of the wall. The new rice shoots are a pleasing green. Is it not because the plants have no feelings?

From the newspaper *Hsin-wen-pao*, May 19th, 1927

Where have they all gone? Why
Is the toad perched on the water-jar, mould sprouting
    on the water-scoop,
Tables, chairs and stools float soaking in the flooded
    fields?
The spiders' stringbridge leads from the east room to
    the west,
The doorway filled with coffins, and the window-
    frames with stones?
How strange and how sad is this scene.
The rust on the sickle has almost mouldered.
Abandoned fishing-nets rot in the ash heaps.

Heavens, cannot even such a village keep them?
There's no end to the open roses; the lotus leaves
    grow like umbrellas;

The rice seedlings are so pointed; and the lake water
  so green;
The sky is so blue; the birdsong rounded like pearls.
Why is the seedling so green? What makes the
  flowers red?
Whose blood is mingled with the earth, whose sweat?
They have gone so decisively, so completely?
What grief did they meet, what vows did they make?
Now can someone tell them, here
The pigs are wandering in the road, the ducks thrust-
  ing amongst the pigs,
The cock is treading on the peonies, the oxen eating
  the cabbage —
Tell them that when the sun has gone down, the
  cattle will not come down the mountain,
Each a black shadow on the ridge waiting.
With the peaks around them like tigers and jackals,
They have looked and shivered.
They all lower their heads and dare not look again.
(Tell them this also.) When they think of the past,
When the night cold approached and white poplars
  shivered in the wind,
They only needed to give a shout at the top of the
  ridge,
When the mountain road was hazardous, the master
  would help them back.
Afterwards the sound of flutes would send them into
  the fold.
How sweet was the hay, how warm the rooms;
When they think about this, a hot tear rolls down
  their cheek,
They press together in a heap, face touching face ...
Go, go tell their masters, tell them,

Tell them everything, keep nothing from them.
Tell them to come back, tell them to come back.
Ask them why they do not even take care of their
    own cattle,
Do they not know that their cattle are just like
    children?
The pitiable cattle are so timid,
Eh – you messenger, where have you gone, too?
Go quickly and tell them, tell Wang the third,
Tell Big Chou and his eight brothers,
Tell the farmers of the Lin-huai-kuan area,
And tell the red-faced blacksmith, old Li,
Tell the one-eyed chap, tell the 'wiseman' Hsü,
Tell Mrs Wang and all the village women,
Tell them all these things, one by one,
Tell them to come back, tell them to come back.
How strange and sad is this scene,
Heavens, cannot even such a village keep them,
Such an Arcadia, yet not a soul to be seen.

Fault

The old man and his load tripped and fell,
The ground was covered with white apricots and red
  cherries,
The old man got up still trembling,
'I know that it was my fault today.'
'You have cut your hand, old man, look.'
'Ai, they've all been bruised, the ripe cherries.'
'Old man, you're not ill, are you?
Why do you stand there lost without a word?'
'I know that it was my fault today,
As soon as it was morning my son kept hurrying me,
My son lay on the bed fuming,
He cursed me for not getting going.

'I knew the day was already late,
But unexpectedly I fell asleep all at once,
What am I to do about this? what am I to do?
When I go home, what shall the whole family have
  for food?'
The old man picked them up and dropped them again,
The ground was covered with white apricots and red
  cherries.

T'ien-an-men*

My God, today I've been scared stiff.
My two legs are still trembling ...
Look, look, they were just about to catch up with me,
Otherwise why should I have run like this?
Sir, let me get my breath back; that thing,
You haven't seen that pitch-black thing,
Headless, lame, so frightening,
Still waving a white flag and talking ...
There's nothing one can do about times like this, you
    ask anyone.
There's nothing really men can do, let alone ghosts.
And they will demonstrate. Can't they mind their
    own business?
You see, they're all somebody's children,
Aren't they just in their teens, what do they do?
Haven't their heads been smashed by guns?
Sir, I heard that yesterday people got killed again,
I bet you it was those idiot students;
At times like this there are really strange happenings.
These students have plenty to eat, to drink –
Last year our uncle was killed at Yang-liu-ch'ing
That was because he was so hungry he had to enlist,
Who is going to send himself to the God of the Dead
    for nothing?

* T'ien-an-men (The Gate of Heavenly Peace) has a square
in front of it where political demonstrations, which some-
times ended in bloodshed, often took place in the early days
of the Republican era.

I've never lied before in my life, I thought
I'd just filled the lamp with oil, a whole jarful,
Why was it that as I was going, suddenly I couldn't
    see the road?
No wonder the bald chap was scared out of his wits
And tells everyone not to go by T'ien-an-men in the
    dark.
So it's bad luck to us rickshaw pullers,
When by tomorrow morning Peking will be full of
    ghosts.

The Song of the Laundry

Laundrying is the commonest occupation of the Chinese in the United States, so many students from China are often asked this question: 'Is your father a laundryman?'

(One, two, three)
Washing clothes they must be washed clean,
(Four, five, six)
Pressing clothes they must be pressed smooth.

I can wash clean handkerchiefs wet with grief,
I can wash white shirts black with guilt.
The grease of greed and the ashes of lust ...
All the dirty things in your house,
Give them to me to wash, give them to me to wash.

Metal smells and blood stinks,
Things that are soiled must be washed clean,
Things that are washed will be soiled again,
You patient people, can you take any notice?
Wash it for them, wash it for them.

You say that the trade of laundryman is too base,
Only the Chinese are willing to descend so low,
Your pastor informs me, saying
Jesus' father was a carpenter by trade,
Do you believe it, do you believe it?

Soapy water cannot produce anything grand,
Washing clothes cannot compare with building
destroyers.

I'll agree that there's no glory in it –
To bathe in blood-like sweat, to wash others' sweat.
Would you do it, would you do it?

Year in, year out, a drop of homesick tears,
In the middle of the night a lamp for washing
    clothes ...
Don't you worry about whether it is base or not,
If it's not clean, if it's not smooth,
Ask the Chinaman, ask the Chinaman.

I can wash clean handkerchiefs wet with grief,
I can wash white shirts black with guilt.
The grease of greed and the ashes of lust ...
All the dirty things in your house,
Give them to me to wash, give them to me to wash.

(One, two, three)
Washing clothes they must be washed clean,
(Four, five, six)
Pressing clothes they must be pressed smooth.

Mr Wen's Desk

Suddenly all the objects started to talk,
Suddenly the desk was bubbling with complaints,
The ink bottle groaned, 'I'm dying of thirst.'
The dictionary shouted that rain was soaking its
    back.

The notepaper cried out that its back was painful from
    bending,
The pen said that ashes were choking its mouth,
The brush said that matches had singed its beard.
The pencil grumbled that the toothbrush lay heavily
    on its leg.

The incense-burner muttered, 'These barbarous books,
One of these days I'll squeeze them off.'
The watch sighed, its bones rusting from sleep.
'There's a wind, there's a wind,' screamed the paper.

The water-holder said that he was specifically for
    water,
How could he stand the stink of tobacco ash?
The table complained that he could hardly get two
    baths a year,
The inkwell said, 'I wash you down every other day.'

'What a master? Who is our master?'
All the objects cursed at once,

'If life is as harassed as this,
It would be better to have no life.'

The master biting on his pipe smiled,
'All creatures should stay in their place,
It is not my intention to ill-treat you,
Orderliness is not within my competence.'

II

from RED CANDLE (1923)

Red Candle

'When the candle turns to ashes the tears begin to dry'
Li Shang-yin

Oh Red Candle!
So red a candle!
Oh Poet!
Spit out your heart and compare
Can the colour be the same?

Oh Red Candle!
Who made the wax – gave you your body?
Who lit the flame – lit your soul?
And why must you burn to ash
Before you release the light?
Mistake on mistake,
Paradox! contradiction!

Oh Red Candle!
There is no mistake, no mistake!
It was to 'burn' out your light –
That was nature's method.

Oh Red Candle!
Since you have been made, then burn!
Burn! burn!
Burn up the dream of men,
Burn up the blood of men –
And save their soul
And break down their prison!

Oh Red Candle!
When the fire of your heart gives light,
Then it is the day for tears to flow.

Oh Red Candle!
The chandler made you
Meaning that you should burn.
Now you are burning
Why break your heart and weep?
Oh I know!
It is the cruel wind come to invade your light,
When you burn unsteadily,
Then in agitation you weep!

Oh Red Candle!
Flow! Why do you not shed tears?
Will you let your flesh
Ceaselessly flow towards men
To cultivate comfort-bringing flowers
And ripen into happy fruit!

Oh Red Candle!
When you weep one tear, part of your heart turns to
    dust.
Heart turned to ash, tears wept are your fate,
To create light is your destiny.

Oh Red Candle!
'Ask not about the harvest, ask about the ploughing.'

from The Death of Li Po

A pair of dragon candles are burnt down to the sticks,
They reborrow the remaining wax from the thick
    tears already shed,
A wasted flame reluctantly flickers on and off,
Panting in the night, trembling uselessly.
Wine-cups and plates strew the table, the wine-jars
    have fallen down in sleep,
The drunken guests have scattered like crows re-
    turning to their nest;
Only the very drunk, drunk like mud, Li Po
(As if his whole body had put itself out of joint)
Sprawls in a crooked heap on a chair in the garden,
Muttering and murmuring, whatever it is he says.

The sound is inaudible, his lips still move ceaselessly;
Suddenly those eyeballs held by red spiders' webs
(They each seem like a miniature drunken man)
Stare for a long time at the timid candle flame :
Just like a hungry lion discovering a small animal,
Soundlessly, its two eyes fix themselves on it;
Then gently and softly it lifts a front foot,
Like lightning anticipating awareness, suddenly
    springs –
So, the candlesticks at the other corners of the table
Are pulled to the floor by this drunkard.

The Western Bank

'He has a lusty spring, when fancy clear
Takes in all beauty with an easy span'

Keats

Here is a river, a great river,
Wide without sides, deep without bottom;
The winds of the four seasons having travelled the
wide world
Return to the river to rest;
A rimless bitter fog is plastered over the whole sky,
And presses on the whole river's endless sound sleep.
Below the bank the river is deep in sleep; above its
banks,
Waves rise unbroken,
Oh, how much pain has been rolled away!
How much happiness has been washed away!
How many hearts have been whipped down by shame
and regret,
With the flash of the eye, fanned up again by vanity!
Whipped down and fanned up,
Or is it buying and selling?
The black night fools deaf and dumb horses and men,
The late tide brought back what the early tide washed
away.
There is no truth, no beauty, no goodness,
Then where do we look for light?

But don't be afraid in the big water
When the waves are so fierce and the water-monsters
so threatening,

It is hard to startle into wakefulness the quiet dreams
    of the mountain grasses,
Amongst the flowers of the rush in the shallow water –
All the same, a man has escaped
The entangled chaotic cage on the river bank.
He saw this great broad, deep water
Which secretly awoke some suspicions :
It clearly is a river with an Eastern Bank
So how can there not be a Western Bank?
Oh, this Eastern Bank's darkness is exactly
The shadow of the light of the Western Bank.

But the endless sound sleep of the whole river
Supports a whole skyful of rimless curtains of fog,
Perhaps there is a Western Bank, but has anyone seen
    it?
Oh … these words are right.
'The evil fog cannot cover me,' the heart said,
'If you can't see, then it is the fault of the eye.'
Sometimes one suddenly sees the thick fog change
Into something thin, floating on the wings of the wind;
Through the cracks in the fog sift
Slivers of golden light scattered on the river's body.
Look! isn't that a huge turtle?
With hairs grown so long!

No, it is a small island
Wearing a headful of plants :
Look, bright fishes and dragons are all coming out
Sunning their shells and combing their beards;
When they have finished grooming, the lovebirds
    thrust their beaks
Into their wings, and sleep.

When the lovebirds sleep, the fishes retreat –
The whole river is desolate;
The sun is listless and rolls up its golden chains
And lets the curtain of fog drop down again :
The evil fog stares at the dead water, everything
Is the same as before.

'Oh, I understand, I never saw
The beauty's face and shape,
I only guessed that the soft movements under the
    brocaded dress
Must be the movements of a beauty's body.
In the same way, what I see is a small island,
What I guess at is the Western Bank!'

'There is an island in the middle of the river, and the
    lamplight
From the Western Bank is cut off by this island.'
These words are everywhere, there are people
Like parrots repeating words they are familiar with,
But the majority of people
Either laugh at his madness or curse him for creating
    rumours.

Some will believe him but still say,
'The Western Bank is not for the people of the Eastern
    Bank.
If it were, why divide them
With a river so wide and deep?'
Some people say, 'The river is too wide and the fog is
    now heavy.
It would be safer to look for a land route to cross.'
There are also people who know

That there is only one road, but just regret that they
    were born wrong –
It is hard to imitate the birds and fly across,
It is hard to imitate the fishes and swim across,
But they are afraid of saying, 'Build a bridge,
Across the island, walk across.' Why?

Snow

The night has scattered countless sky blossoms like
    down
Woven into a huge cloak,
Lightly wrapping the worn world
From head to foot :
Then added a dead man's shroud.

It buried scale-like roofs of houses
But couldn't bury the thread of blue smoke from the
    roofs.
Oh, sinuous smoke !
Like a poet's soul stretching up,
Piercing his body's shell, making straight for paradise.

The arrogant long-stepping wind and frost trod on the
    world,
The deep forest's trembling crowd, after battling long,
See at last the white cloak,
They all cry out in joy, 'Peace is here, our struggle is
    victorious !
Is this not winter's white flag of surrender ?'

Evening

The sun after working hard all day
Has earned a peaceful evening,
His whole face is red with pleasure
Intent on running to the valley in one breath.

Darkness can be compared with soundless drizzle;
Slowly floating down upon the whole world ...
The sleepy love-grass folds up its green hair and bends
    its soft neck,
The street-lamps steal the colours of the setting sun
    and change them into golden flowers;
Leaving only the fountain
Not caring about breaking others' deep dreams
Laughs loudly as before in gaiety, playing by itself.
Strollers after the evening meal
Are just like a swarm of honey-filled bees,
In threes and fives they are all
In the streets, flying about the railings of the bridge.
Ong ... ong ... ong ... listen to what they sing.

        About the beauty of flowers?
        Or the richness of the taste of honey?
        About the tyranny of the queen?
        Or the cruelty of the east wind?

Oh, mysterious evening!
I ask, this unfathomable song of yours,
This noisy clamorous crowd,
Whose song contains your real meaning?

A Poet

People say that I am a little like a star,
However bright can only be the companion of the
   moon,
And never as useful as lamps –
They shine on the world working, and not only to
   please the eye.

People say that the spring wind sets me alight, with
   flowers like fire,
Another puff, and I shall become a heap of dead ashes,
Leaving behind leaves like armour, prickles like hor-
   nets' stings,
Who would dare to take them to his naked bosom?

Some people also compare me with a far-away
   mountain,
But they would rather look on my colours from afar
And never believe that in the depth of the white
   cloud
There is another world – a heavenly kingdom.

The others perhaps say this, perhaps that,
But no one has the right answer.
'Thank you, friends,' I say, 'don't bother about me,
You are so busy, who has thoughts to spare for me?

'In the middle of your busyness, when you feel the
   suffocating heat,

A breeze comes, you drink it down unthinking,
There is no need to ask who sent it,
But just feel naturally that its coming is timely.'

Looking Back

Nine years of Tsinghua life,
A glance behind –
It is the desert of an autumn night,
But showing one glow-worm,
Growing brighter as one looks,
On four sides is the murky endlessness of desolate
   darkness.
This is the dark-red and tender green season of late
   spring:
Now if we go to the Lotus Pond –
The weight of loneliness presses down so hard on the
   water
That not a ripple moves on the surface –
Dead silence!
Suddenly the silent spirit has departed,
The mirror breaks,
Each of us gasps.
Look! The laughing flames of the sun – a ray of
   golden light –
Sift past the gaps in the trees, scattering on my fore-
   head;
Today the charioteer of the sun has crowned me,
I am master of the universe.

Defeat

Once I cultivated a bowl of rare flowers
And with difficulty produced one bud,
But half open, half shut, it would never bloom.
I lost my patience from waiting, and forcibly opened
    it up,
Then day by day it withered, withered pitiably.
Now I wanted it to close up again but it could not.
In the end I never managed to see the flower I wanted
    to see.

Once I dreamt a rare dream,
I kept thinking that it was too misty,
I didn't care, and let it be broken;
I woke, and waited right till the moon set, waited till
    the day dawned,
To weave a new dream, but since I could not,
And could not repair the old one either,
In the end I never dreamt the dream I wanted.

Rhapsodical Thoughts

In the silence of the evening,
Out of my desolate brain,
Strange thoughts often come bursting out,
Aberrant thoughts;

Like in front of an old temple,
Out of a belfry locked by dust drenched by rain,
Fly a crowd of suspicious bats,
Small monsters neither bird nor mammal.

Like an ambitious bat,
My thoughts will not crawl along the ground,
But always wheel in rings in the air,
Circles, ovals, all kinds of rings.

Out of my desolate brain
In the silence of the evening,
Often strange thoughts break out
Just like those bats.

I am a young, strong exile

I am a young, strong exile,
I don't know what crime I have been guilty of.

It was evening,
They pushed me out of doors,
The red doors of happiness were shut upon me,
The golden-armoured, purple-faced gods of the gate*
Raised their swords to chase me;
I could only rush into the deep darkness,
Ploughing my way forward.

Suddenly there were the upturned eaves of a fine
    mansion,
Like the wings of a fabulous bird
Poised upon the frothy surface of the sea;
Through the crossed lattice of the window
Flooded an intoxicating lamplight, as strong as yel-
    low wine;
And a mournful, passionate music of flute and song
Made restless by the pursuing castanets
Screwed itself like a gimlet into my heart :
My body unconsciously became half its weight,
As though it was dancing before those peacock
    screens.

Oh happiness – fearful happiness –

* Paper images of gods in armour were often pasted on the
doorposts of Chinese homes to protect them from evil.

Unsheathed its sarcastic silver sword
And pierced me awake;
Oh, then I knew
That I had been a sinner against happiness
And exiled from the palace of joy,
How can I linger round here aimlessly?

Off! Let me walk again towards that endless black
    road!
Oh, but I am too severely wounded;
My steps get gradually heavier,
My fresh life-blood
Gradually dyes the withered grass at my feet.

I am a young, strong exile,
I don't know what crime I have been guilty of.

The Last Day of Autumn

Drinking hard the whole night through with the West
    Wind.
He is now drunk, unsteady in his head and on his
    feet;
Scattering gold and ripping brocaded silk,
Still noisily crying.

Extravagant autumn, nature's profligate!
Spring and summer have laboured for half the year
How much can they have hoarded up
For you to squander it like this?
Now you must be bankrupt.

Rotten Fruit

My flesh has long since been chewed by black worms.
I sleep on the cold stinging green moss,
Willingly letting rot add to rot,
Only waiting for it to pierce my shell,
For rot to break down my prison,
My shut-in soul
Wearing a pea-green vest will then
Smilingly jump out.

The Stream

The lead-grey tree shadows
Are a long nightmare,
Lying across the sleeping
Stream's breast.
The stream struggles, struggles ...
As though without the slightest effect.

Colours

Life was a piece of worthless white paper;
Ever since green gave me growth,
Red gave me passion,
Yellow taught me loyalty,
Blue taught me purity,
Pink gave me hope,
Grey gave me sadness;
To finish this many-coloured painting
Black will add death.
After this
I pamper my life
Because I love its colours.

from Scarlet Beads*

10

We are one body!
Our union
Is as round and perfect as the globe.
But you are the Eastern hemisphere,
And I the western,
The tears that we ourselves have shed
Made this vast Pacific,
Cutting us in two.

14

I send these poems to you,
Even if you do not know all the words,
It doesn't matter.
With your fingers you can
Gently caress them,
Like a doctor feeling a patient's pulse,
Perhaps you can detect in
Their excited pulsations
The same rhythm as your own heart-beats.

19

I am a lone swan startled by arrows,
My mouth wants to shout for you,

* *Abrus precatorius*, small round beads from a leguminous
plant, symbols of love in China; sometimes known in the
West as 'rosary beads'.

But it must clench the rushes,
To protect my life.
I am so harassed.

26

Do you understand?
We are a pair of red candles
Shining on a wedding feast for guests;
We stand at opposite corners
Of the table,
Quietly burning away our lives,
Companions to their pleasure.
When they have eaten,
Our lives will have burnt away.

42

I have sung all kinds of songs,
But you alone I have forgotten.
The more I sing the more my songs should grow
    newer and lovelier.
In these last and loveliest songs,
                Each word is a pearl,
                Each word a tear,
My queen!
Let me make amends with these gifts,
These I offer you on my knees.

III

Wonder

What I wanted was never the fire-equal red, or the
    black
At midnight of the Peach Blossom Lake,* or the plain-
    tiveness of the ancient lute,
Or the scent of the briar roses; I have never whole-
    heartedly loved the pride of the spotted leopard,
The tender beauty I wanted was not that possessed
    by any white dove.
What I wanted was never any of these, but the crys-
    tallization of these,
The Wonder ten thousand times more marvellous!
But this soul was desperate with hunger and I could
    not
Let it go short of nourishment. Then, even if it was
    only chaff and bran
One must beg for it like alms. Heaven knows I don't
    behave like this
Willingly. I was not stubborn, or stupid,
I got tired of waiting, waiting in vain for the Wonder
    to arrive.
I dared not let my soul go short of nourishment; who
    can say
That a treeful of sounding cicadas, a jar of unstrained
    wine is much?
Even mountain ranges, the light on ravines or the
    glittering starry emptiness

* A very deep lake in Anhwei.

Are all so commonplace, so unutterably common-
place, not worth
The helpless happy surprise that shouts the most
moving names,
The longing to carve them in gold and put them into
a song.
I also say that to let tears come at the song of the
oriole
Is rather too absurd, too unconvincing, simply not
worthwhile.
But perhaps I couldn't help being like that : this heart
Was really desperate with hunger, I had to be
economical and pretend that wild roots
Were fine cooking.
        There is no harm in saying it out loud if only –
If only the Wonder will show its face, I shall aban-
don the commonplace instantly,
I shall never again look at a leaf outlined by frost and
dream of the glory of spring flowers,
Never waste again this soul's strength, but I shall peel
open the uncut stone
And look for the warmth of the white jade inside.
Show me the Wonder
And I shall never again whip 'ugliness', forcing it to
give up
The meaning of what is behind; really I have long
grown tired
Of these things, these misunderstandings that are
really too hard to explain.
All I want is one clear word, flashing like a holy sign
With sacred light, I want it whole, the beauty of its
full face.
I am not stubborn, I am not stupid, I cannot see the

Round fan without envisaging the immortal face be-
hind the fan.
Then
    I shall wait, no matter for how many incarnations –
Since I have made a vow at the beginning, I don't
    know how many
Incarnations ago – I have been waiting, I don't com-
    plain, only wait quietly
For the Wonder to arrive. There must be such a day,
Let lightning strike at me, volcanoes consume me, all
    hell rise up
And assault me … Fear? Don't worry, in any case the
    whirlwind
Will not blow out the lamp of my soul. I wish this
    body would turn to ashes,
It won't matter, because that, that will be my momen-
    tary,
My one momentary instant of infinity – a puff of
    fragrance, the most mysterious
Silence (sun, moon, all movements of stars long since
Halted, time too stopped), the most rounded peace …
I hear the squeak of the hinge on the door
Bringing with it the rustle of a skirt – that would be
    the Wonder –
In the half-open golden door, wearing a circle of light,
    You.

1899   Born in Hupei, China.

1913–22   At Tsinghua College, Peking.

1922   Married to Miss Kao Hsiao-chen, a school teacher from his native town in Hupei. The marriage was arranged by their families.

1922   Set sail for the United States, leaving his wife in China.

1922–3   At the Chicago Institute of Art.

1923–4   At Colorado College, Colorado Springs.

1923   *Red Candle* published.

1924   At New York, entered at the Arts Student League of New York, but attended no classes.

1925   Returned to China to be Dean of the new Institute of Art in Peking.

1927   Spent one term at the Wu-sung Political Academy.

1927   At Sun Yat-sen University, Nanking.

1928   *Dead Water* published.

Spent one term at Wu-han University.

1929–32   At Ch'ing-tao University.

1932   Joined staff of Tsinghua University, Peking.

1937   At the beginning of the Sino-Japanese war was evacuated to the interior of China where he eventually settled at Kunming, Yünnan.

1943   Joined the People's Democratic League.

1945   Armistice: reopening of universities and return of students to their homes.

1946   Assassinated at Kunming.

CAPE EDITIONS

1 The Scope of Anthropology, Claude Lévi-Strauss
2 Call me Ishmael, Charles Olson
3 Writing Degree Zero, Roland Barthes
4 Elements of Semiology, Roland Barthes
5 I Wanted to Write a Poem, William Carlos Williams
6 The Memorandum, Václav Havel
7 The Selected Poems of Nazim Hikmet
8 Lichtenberg: Aphorisms & Letters
9 Tango, Slawomir Mrozek
10 On Love ... Aspects of a Single Theme, José Ortega y Gasset
11 Manhood, Michel Leiris
12 Bees: Their Vision, Chemical Senses, and Language, Karl von Frisch
13 Lunar Caustic, Malcolm Lowry
14 Twenty Prose Poems, Charles Baudelaire
15 Journeys, Günter Eich
16 A Close Watch on the Trains, Bohumil Hrabal
17 Mayan Letters, Charles Olson
18 The Courtship Habits of the Great Crested Grebe, Julian Huxley
19 The Supermale, Alfred Jarry
20 Poems & Antipoems, Nicanor Parra
21 In Praise of Krishna: Songs from the Bengali
22 History Will Absolve Me, Fidel Castro
23 Selected Poems, Georg Trakl
24 Selected Poems, Yves Bonnefoy
25 Ferdinand, Louis Zukofsky
26 The Recluse, Adalbert Stifter
27 Dialectical Materialism, Henri Lefebvre
29 Soul on Ice, Eldridge Cleaver
30 The Human Sciences and Philosophy, Lucien Goldmann
31 Selected Poems, André Breton
32 Soap, Francis Ponge
33 Histoire Extraordinaire, Michel Butor
34 Conversations with Claude Lévi-Strauss, G. Charbonnier
35 An Absence, Uwe Johnson

36 A Critique of Pure Tolerance, Robert Paul Wolff, Barrington Moore Jr, Herbert Marcuse
37 The Garden Party, Václav Havel
38 Twenty Love Poems and a Song of Despair, Pablo Neruda
39 Genesis as Myth and Other Essays, Edmund Leach
40 Cold Mountain, Han-shan
41 The World, the Flesh and the Devil, J. D. Bernal
42 The Death of Lysanda, Yitzhak Orpaz
43 How Are Verses Made? Vladimir Mayakovsky
44 Although, Miroslav Holub
45 Scrolls: Selected Poems, Nikolai Zabolotsky
46 Poems, Hermann Hesse
47 Selected Poems, Ondra Lysohorsky
48 Chamber Music, James Joyce
49 The Increased Difficulty of Concentration, Václav Havel
50 Vatzlav, Slawomir Mrozek
51 Claude Lévi-Strauss: An Introduction, Octavio Paz